Looking Good

HAIR

by Arlene C. Rourke

Rourke Publications, Inc.
Vero Beach, FL 32964

The author wishes to thank the following people for their help in the preparation of this book:

Dixie Montegomery, owner and director of a modeling school and agency.

Eileen Griffin, artist, illustrator and owner of a graphic arts company.

Library of Congress Cataloging in Publication Data

Rourke, Arlene, 1944-
    Hair.

    Bibliography: p.
    Includes index.
    Summary: Tips for hair care, from finding a hair-dresser and choosing a hairstyle to setting and coloring hair.
    1. Hair—Care and hygiene—Juvenile literature.
2. Hairdressing—Juvenile literature.   3. Beauty, Personal—Juvenile literature.   [1. Hair—Care and hygiene.   2. Beauty, Personal]   I. Title.
RL91.R83   1986   646.7'24   86-17833
ISBN 0-86625-278-9

CONTENTS

BEAUTIFUL HAIR

There is a reason why hair is called a woman's "crowning glory." Beautiful, shining hair is a pleasure to see. It is a major beauty asset and is well worth the care you put into it.

If you are a brunette you have approximately 100,000 hairs growing from your scalp. If you're a blonde you tend to have more; you redheads have a bit less.

Hair grows about ½" a month. Of course, that can vary due to general health, diet, age and climate. A child's hair tends to grow faster than an adult's. It also tends to be lighter. If you were very blonde as a child, you might notice that your hair will darken as you become a teenager.

Some people worry when they see strands of hair in their brushes or combs. Don't be concerned. It's perfectly normal to lose between 50 to 100 hairs a day.

Sun, dyes and permanents are the major enemies of your hair. Use them in moderation. The sun is a special villain. It dries up the natural moisturizers in both your hair and your skin. If you're a sun worshipper — as many of us are — protect your hair. Use hats and scarves when you're at the beach or pool. Don't forget to use conditioner.

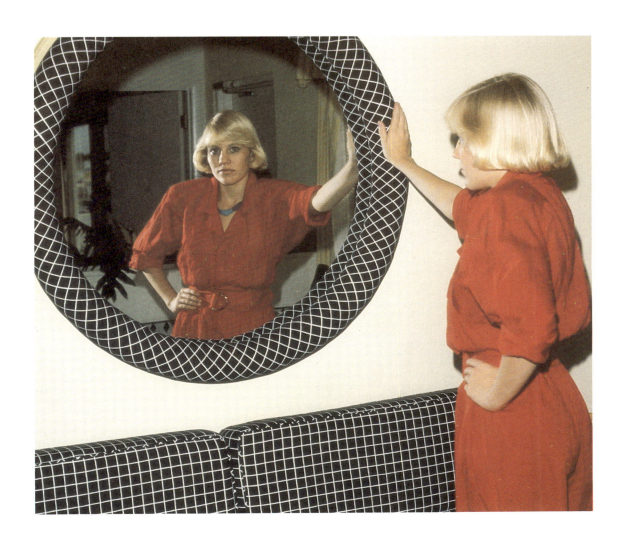

CROSS SECTION OF HAIR SHAFT

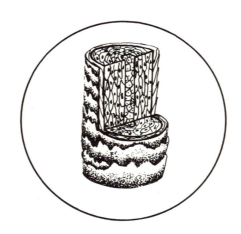

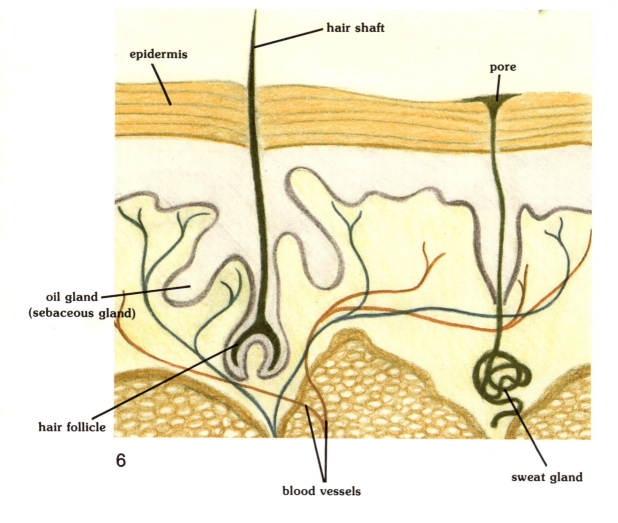

hair shaft

epidermis

pore

oil gland
(sebaceous gland)

hair follicle

sweat gland

blood vessels

6

What Makes Up Hair

Hairs grow out of hair follicles. The hair cells begin to grow at the root and push toward the scalp as new cells form underneath. The oil (sebaceous) glands secrete oil into the hair shaft. This keeps the hair soft and shining.

What makes hair beautiful?
    Color
    Texture
    Volume
    Shine
    Cut

Color depends on the amount of melanin (brown-black pigment) that you have in your body. More melanin results in darker hair, less melanin in lighter hair.

Texture depends on the shape of the hair. Straight hairs have a round shape. Wavy or curly hairs are flat.

Volume is the overall look of "fullness" that your hair has. Most people strive for a bouncy, "lots of hair" look.

Shine depends on the way you care for your hair. Use the right hair products for your type of hair. Eat the right foods. Get lots of exercise and sleep.

Cut can accent good features and hide bad ones. Get a good hairdresser (more on this later) and have your hair cut regularly.

NORMAL HAIR

Getting to Know Your Hair

Your hair and scalp probably fall into one of three categories:

Normal
Dry
Oily

Normal hair is healthy, bouncy, soft and shiny. It takes a set well. With a good cut, it is easy to manage.

Probably the word "normal" is inaccurate, since most people do *not* have perfect hair. Some hair is too dry and needs extra conditioning. Many teenagers tend to have oily hair. This is because of the hormonal changes taking place in their bodies. Extra oil is secreted by the oil glands. This oil collects on the scalp and hair, making them greasy.

Most people need some help with their hair, so don't be discouraged if you do too.

TIP: A three inch strand of hair is about six months old. That's a lot of shampooing, sunning, and setting. For your hair's sake, get it cut every four to six weeks.

DRY HAIR

Do you have. . . . . . .

    flyaway hair
    flaking scalp
    dandruff
    split ends
You have dry hair.

Dry hair is caused by:

insufficient production of oil by the oil glands
overexposure to the sun
drying shampoos
frequent use of blow dryers and hot rollers
hard chemicals, such as chlorine, permanents
    or hair colors

What to do for dry hair:

use a shampoo rich in conditioners
only one sudsing per shampoo, if possible
rinse thoroughly
after shampooing, use a conditioner
let hair dry naturally
use a headcover outdoors
rinse pool water and perspiration out immediately
go easy on hair spray
use a deep conditioner once a week
trim split ends

TIP: Before going to the pool or the beach put conditioner on your hair. The heat from the sun will give you the maximum benefit from it.

TIP: Wet hair with clear water *before* going in the pool. Wet hair absorbs less chlorine.

OILY HAIR

Do you have. . . . . . .
  greasy, limp hair
  stringy hair
  flat hair with no volume to it
You have oily hair.

Oily hair is caused by:

overproduction of oil in the oil glands
stress
hot, humid climate
hormonal changes

What to do for oily hair:

shampoo frequently, concentrate on the scalp
use water based hair products
avoid products with oil
keep combs and brushes clean
avoid tight hair coverings, scalp needs to breathe
wear your hair in a simple style

TIP: Avoid harsh shampoos. They tend to be irritating. Oil based shampoos make the hair greasier. Use a shampoo formulated for oily hair.

Don't "overbrush" your hair. Vigorous, frequent brushing stimulates the oil glands to produce more oil. You don't need that.

Protect your hair in the sun. Don't think that because your hair has lots of oil it can't be damaged. It certainly can.

FINDING A GOOD HAIRDRESSER

A good haircut is essential to the health and beauty of your hair. No hairstyle will look its best without a good cut. The first step on the road to a great hairstyle is finding the right hairdresser.

How do you find a good hairdresser? Ask around. If you admire a friend's hairstyle, ask her who cut it. If you see a stranger in school with a great cut, tell her you like it. Most people love compliments. Then ask her who her hairdresser is.

When you've lined up a hairdresser call his salon and make an appointment. Don't just breeze in off the street and expect him to take you. Good hairdressers have tight schedules and cannot fit people in at the last moment.

Make an appointment for a time of day when you are not rushed. You will need to talk with him before he works on your hair.

Be on time for your appointment. Don't go immediately into the back room and change into a robe. Make sure your hairdresser sees you in your street clothes *before* your hair is wet. A good hairdresser wants to see what his client looks like in her "normal" life. In that way he can judge what style is suitable for you.

He may ask you questions. How do you style your hair at home? Are you good with your hair or are you "all thumbs"? How much time and energy do you have to devote to your hair? What are your interests and hobbies?

If you're the athletic type you probably shampoo frequently. In that case you don't want a fussy style that takes a lot of care. Also, if you're "all thumbs" you don't want an elaborate style that you can't handle.

It helps if you bring a picture of the style you think you would like. Understand that you might not have the type of hair or the right face shape to carry that style. Be open to suggestions. Don't expect to look *exactly* like a beautiful model in a picture. It almost never works out that way.

You may want to ask *him* questions. Why is he recommending a particular style? How would you care for it? What are his rates?

Do you feel relaxed and comfortable with him? Do you think that he is trying to push something on you that you don't want or need?

TIP: Don't let a hairdresser do anything drastic to your hair on your first visit. Try him out on a shampoo and blow dry. If you like the result, you'll probably approve of his hairstyling.

CHOOSING A HAIRSTYLE

How can you find the right hairstyle for you? Study your body.

What is your *height*, *weight* and *bone structure*? The style you choose should be in proportion to your *total* body. Example: If you are tall and overweight a "pixie" hairdo will not look good on you.

What is the *texture* of your hair? Do you have fine or coarse hair? Even the best style will not work on hair that is the wrong texture for it. Example: a style requiring lots of body will go limp on baby fine hair.

What are your *good* and *bad features*? Would a different hairstyle lessen the bad ones and accentuate the good ones?

How much *time*, *money* and *energy* are you prepared to spend on your hair?

What is the shape of your face? *Face shape* is one of the most important points to consider in choosing a hairstyle. Study the face shapes on the following pages and find the style that is best for you.

OVAL FACE

An oval face can carry most hairstyles.

ROUND FACE

You need height, little volume on the sides.

18

SQUARE FACE

Never cut your hair right at the jawline.
It makes your face look even more square.

TRIANGULAR FACE

Emphasize angles. Try different types of bangs.

LONG FACE

You need width at the sides, not on top.

CARING FOR YOUR HAIR

Shampooing is the most common treatment you will give your hair. Most people shampoo two or three times a week. If you have oily hair you will want to shampoo more often. Keeping your face and scalp clean will also help control acne.

Tips on Shampooing:

1 — Choose a shampoo that is right for your hair type: normal, dry or oily.
2 — Before shampooing, be sure your hair is free of tangles.
3 — Rinse well. Soap will leave your hair dry and dull.
4 — Final rinse should be with cold water. It makes your hair shine!
5 — Never use a brush to untangle wet hair. Hair is weak when it is wet. It breaks easily. Instead, use a wide-toothed comb.

How to Shampoo Your Hair:

1 — Massage scalp with fingers to improve circulation.

2 — Wet hair with warm
water. Apply shampoo.

3 — Work up lather.
Concentrate on hairline.

4 — Rinse thoroughly
with cold water.
Repeat shampooing if
necessary.

How to Condition Your Hair

If you use a commercial conditioner follow the directions. Usually, you will be told to apply the conditioner evenly over your hair and leave it on a few minutes. Rinse it off thoroughly.

If your hair is very dry or damaged you may need a deep conditioner. Deep conditioners take about 30 minutes to work. For best results, wrap your hair in a warm towel and sit in the sun or under a warm dryer. If you have dry hair, deep conditioning should be done about once a week.

Things to remember about conditioning your hair:

1 — Use a conditioner formulated for your type of hair.

2 — Don't "overcondition." Too much conditioning will leave your hair limp and hard to set.

3 — You can make a simple, inexpensive conditioner using kitchen oils, such as sesame, mayonaisse or olive. Just warm the oil and apply it to your hair. Warning: Oil is very difficult to wash out and it tends to darken blonde hair.

STYLING YOUR HAIR

There are so many products on the market to assist you in styling your hair. It is difficult to wade through all of them. Here's a rundown of the tools of the trade and some helpful hints on hairstyling.

The Tools

Combs and brushes Look for rounded tips. They will not cut into your scalp. Choose natural bristle brushes. They're easier on your hair. Wash them once a week.

> **TIP:** Black girls' hair tends to be especially fragile. Avoid picks or other sharp tools.

Rollers Non-electric rollers are used when the hair is wet or damp. Apply a setting lotion, comb through, set, and dry.

Hot rollers Use hot rollers only when your hair is *completely* dry. Use only setting lotions especially designed for hot rollers or curling irons.

Curling irons They work on the same principles as hot rollers. They are easier to travel with and are handy for quick touch-ups.

Blow dryers Get a blow dryer with several heat settings. If you're just drying your hair, use the lowest setting. For styling, use the hottest setting. Always keep the dryer moving.

TIP: Heat is an enemy of your hair. Use hot rollers, curling irons and blow dryers *sparingly* or you'll wind up with frizz instead of great looking hair.

Mousse Shake the can and pump a *small* amount into your palm. Rub your palms together and spread the mousse evenly through your hair. Style with a curling iron, hot rollers or fingers.

Gels Gels are good for achieving a more "fixed" look or for special effects. For example, styles that call for the hair to stick out straight need a gel.

Hair sprays Sprays help keep your set in place. If you use spray, it will be the last thing you apply to your hair. Go easy on spray. It coats the hair.

TIP: Beauty salons often mark up the price on products they sell. Make a list of your hair care needs and find a beauty supply outlet. You can get everything from hair spray to hot rollers at a reduced price!

28

Special effects

Some people are unhappy with the color or texture of their hair. They try coloring or permanenting or straightening in order to achieve the hairstyle they want.

These special treatments greatly alter your appearance and the composition of your hair. Do not color, permanent or straighten your hair as a lark. Give it a great deal of thought. *Be sure your parents approve.* You will be permanently changing your hair. If you don't like it, you may have to wait months for it to grow out.

Coloring involves dyeing or bleaching your hair to the desired color. Dyes and bleaches cannot be washed out. There are some temporary tints which do wash out. You might want to try them for parties or proms.

Permanents chemically change the texture of your hair. They give limp hair body and volume. Good permanents are not frizzy. Remember to deep condition afterward. Permanents are hard on hair.

Straighteners or curl relaxers are used by some black women and girls. Relaxers work like permanents — only in reverse. They take the curl *out* of your hair. As with permanents, always condition afterward.

> **TIP:** Have special treatments done by a hairdresser and save yourself a lot of tears.

BIBLIOGRAPHY

All About Hair, Herbert S. Feinberg, M.D. Wallingford Press, Alpine, New Jersey.

Healthy Hair and Common Sense, Dale Alexander. Witkower Press, Inc. West Hartford, Connecticut.

Family Circle Guide to Beauty, Mary Milo. New York Times Company Publications, New York.

The Make-over: A Teen's Guide to Looking and Feeling Beautiful, Jane Parks-McKay. William Morrow and Company, Inc. New York.

"Hair," Vogue Magazine. July 1986, pps. 208-215.

"What a Difference a Trim Makes," Seventeen. February 1986, p. 110.

"Hair That Fits Your Face," Seventeen. September 1985, p. 154.

Superhair, Jonathan Zizmor. Berkley Publishing Corporation, distributed by G.P. Putnam's Sons, New York.

The AMA Book of Skin and Hair Care, Linda Allen Schoen. Lippincott Company, Philadelphia and New York.

Being Beautiful, Carolyn Meyer. William Morrow and Company, New York.

"Lush Summer Hair," Seventeen. June 1986, p. 134.

INDEX